HIROSHIMA

John Hersey

TECHNICAL DIRECTOR Maxwell Krohn
EDITORIAL DIRECTOR Justin Kestler
MANAGING EDITOR Ben Florman

SERIES EDITORS Boomie Aglietti, Justin Kestler
PRODUCTION Christian Lorentzen

WRITERS Brendan Gibbon, Alexa Gutheil
EDITORS Benjamin Morgan, Karen Schrier, John Crowther

This edition published by Spark Publishing

Spark Publishing
A Division of SparkNotes LLC
120 Fifth Avenue, 8th Floor
New York, NY 10011

02 03 04 05 SN 9 8 7 6 5 4 3 2 1

Please send all comments and questions or report errors to
feedback@sparknotes.com.

Library of Congress information available upon request

Printed and bound in the United States

RRD-C

ISBN 1-58663-521-2

INTRODUCTION: STOPPING TO BUY SPARKNOTES ON A SNOWY EVENING

Whose words these are you *think* you know.
Your paper's due tomorrow, though;
We're glad to see you stopping here
To get some help before you go.

Lost your course? You'll find it here.
Face tests and essays without fear.
Between the words, good grades at stake:
Get great results throughout the year.

Once school bells caused your heart to quake
As teachers circled each mistake.
Use SparkNotes and no longer weep,
Ace every single test you take.

Yes, books are lovely, dark, and deep,
But only what you grasp you keep,
With hours to go before you sleep,
With hours to go before you sleep.

CONTENTS

––––––––––––––––––

NOTE: This SparkNote uses the Vintage edition, which was published in 1985. Editions of *Hiroshima* published before 1985 do not include the fifth chapter, which was written forty years after the original edition.

CONTEXT

J OHN HERSEY (1914–1993) GREW UP in both China and the United States and graduated from Yale in 1936. One of his first jobs was working as a secretary for prominent author Sinclair Lewis. From 1939 to 1945, he served as a war correspondent for *Time* magazine; during that time he wrote two popular books about American troops in Asia, *Men on Bataan* and *Into the Valley.* Hersey's third book, *A Bell for Adano* (1944), a novel about the U.S. army in Italy, won the Pulitzer Prize. After the enormous success of *Hiroshima,* published in 1946, Hersey continued to write both nonfiction and fiction, although none of his later writings attained the status of his earlier works. He taught at Yale, MIT, and the American Academy in Rome, and became actively involved in politics. He was a vocal opponent of America's involvement in Vietnam. In 1985 Hersey released a new edition of *Hiroshima* with a lengthy postscript detailing the lives of its six major figures in the forty years since the bomb.

From 1945 to 1946, Hersey visited Japan on a trip sponsored by *Life* magazine and the *New Yorker,* to write about the people of Hiroshima in the aftermath of the atomic bomb. The editors of the *New Yorker* originally planned to include his account in serial form over a number of issues. After they read the entire manuscript, they decided at the last minute—too late to change the peaceful scene already placed on the cover—to devote an unprecedented entire issue to Hersey's story.

The issue's publication on August 31, 1946, caused a near frenzy of activity. It sold out in just a few hours, and the *New Yorker* was overwhelmed with requests for reprints. The magazine, which normally sold for fifteen cents, was scalped for fifteen to twenty dollars. Other ways of reproducing the text quickly sprang up—the Book-of-the-Month Club distributed free copies, and the text was read in its entirety on national radio. Albert Einstein ordered 1,000 copies of the magazine, but his order could not be filled. The book was quickly translated into many different languages and distributed around the world, though not in Japan, because of American censorship.

Most reviewers hailed *Hiroshima* as an instant classic, praising Hersey's calm narrative and vivid characterizations. Some people worried that the book would make Americans too sympathetic to the Japanese, but many—even those who were staunch supporters of the bomb—agreed that Hersey helped to penetrate the cloud of complacency that had developed in America regarding use of the atomic bomb. Before the book, anti-Japanese feeling was still rampant, and stereotypes of the Japanese as fanatical or sadistic people were very much a part of the American psyche. The American public was ignorant in many ways about just how destructive the bomb was; photographs from Hiroshima focused on property damage, and statistics about the loss of life hardly told the entire story. Many prominent military leaders had attributed the heavy loss of life in Hiroshima to faulty construction of homes or ruptured gas mains. *Hiroshima* put a human face on the numbers and showed Americans why the atomic bomb was so devastating. Furthermore, because *Hiroshima* detailed the lives of six characters in depth, it showed Americans that ordinary Japanese citizens were not really different from them.

In the years since its publication, *Hiroshima* has remained an extremely important work. Recently, New York University's School of Journalism ranked it the number one work of journalism of the twentieth century. The book has its critics, however; there are some who feel that Hersey's impartiality leaves him no room for moral judgments and that the book does not inspire any kind of real outrage about America's use of nuclear weapons. Indeed, there is little indication that the book inspired much protest or criticism of Truman and the American government at the time. Many readers believed that the bomb had to be controlled, but they did not dispute its effectiveness in ending the war with Japan. As a result, there is a vocal minority who accuse Hersey of a significant irresponsibility, because he did not express enough moral outrage about the bomb along with the horrific images he relates; nor did he suggest that the bomb was unnecessary for ending the war. Hersey has said that he felt both despair and relief when he heard that the bomb had been dropped. Because he grew up in China, and saw Japanese atrocities while at Guadalcanal and Bataan, it is likely that he was not completely sympathetic to the Japanese cause.

PLOT OVERVIEW

O N AUGUST 6, 1945, the American army decimates the city of Hiroshima with a bomb of enormous power; out of a population of 250,000, the bomb kills nearly 100,000 people and injures 100,000 more. In its original edition, Hersey's *Hiroshima* traces the lives of six survivors—two doctors, two women, and two religious men—from the moment the bomb drops until a few months later. In 1985, Hersey added a postscript that now forms the book's fifth chapter. In this chapter, Hersey reexamines these six individuals' lives in the forty years since the bomb.

The Reverend Mr. Kiyoshi Tanimoto, a community leader and an American-educated Methodist pastor, is uninjured by the explosion. As fires spread around the city, he helps get people to safety at a small park on the outskirts of the city. Tanimoto is aided by Father Wilhelm Kleinsorge, a Jesuit priest. Despite his own illness, Father Kleinsorge consoles the wounded and brings water to those who need it. Many of the victims are too weak or wounded to move, and in the absence of any official help, people like Father Kleinsorge and Mr. Tanimoto are left to protect them from encroaching fires, whirlwinds, and the rising tide of the river. Among the victims they help are Mrs. Hatsuyo Nakamura and her young children.

Miss Toshiko Sasaki is a young clerk whose leg is fractured in the blast. Her wound becomes terribly infected, and she receives no real medical help for weeks after the explosion. The bomb kills more than half the doctors in Hiroshima and injures most of the rest; Dr. Masakazu Fujii, for instance, is unable to help anybody but himself for a long while. Dr. Terufumi Sasaki, on the other hand, remains the only uninjured doctor on the staff of the Red Cross Hospital, and in the months after the explosion he barely leaves his post, trying to stem the tide of death rising around him.

Weeks after the explosion, after Japan capitulates and Hiroshima begins to rebuild, a new terror strikes: radiation sickness. Victims become nauseated, feverish, and anemic; many people, such as Mrs. Nakamura, watch their hair fall out. The disease baffles everyone, and many, including Father Kleinsorge, never fully recover. Still, the people of Hiroshima try to return to their normal lives. In his added postscript, Hersey traces the lives of these six characters in the forty years after the atomic bomb. Father Kleinsorge and Dr. Fujii die from sudden illnesses years later. Mrs. Nakamura and Miss Sasaki scrape their way up from the bottom to become happy and successful. After working hard and supporting her family, Mrs. Nakamura lives comfortably on a pension and a government allowance, and Miss Sasaki becomes a nun. Dr. Sasaki and Mr. Tanimoto devote their lives to helping people. Mr. Tanimoto in particular plays an important role in trying to help the victims of the bomb—most notably the Hiroshima Maidens, whose burns are so bad that they require plastic surgery. He becomes a minor celebrity in America and somewhat unsuccessfully tries to spread a message of peace in a time of nuclear escalation.

In the end, Hersey finds that the horrors of nuclear war are far from over—the citizens of Hiroshima still suffer from aftereffects, and nuclear escalation continues to threaten the entire world. Hersey also finds that these six people show, in the aftermath of the bomb and the war, remarkable feelings of good will, reconciliation, and pride.

CHARACTER LIST

Mrs. Hatsuyo Nakamura A tailor's widow living in Hiroshima. Mrs. Nakamura narrowly escapes disaster when the explosion destroys her house. She and her three children cope with illness and radiation poisoning for years after the bomb, and she faces tremendous difficulties finding work and housing in the years after the explosion.

Dr. Terufumi Sasaki A young surgeon at the Red Cross Hospital in Hiroshima. Dr. Sasaki treats thousands of the dying and wounded after the bomb, and eventually operates on Miss Sasaki's fractured and infected leg. After the war, he studies radiation sickness and other effects of the bomb.

Father Wilhelm Kleinsorge A German Jesuit priest living in Hiroshima. Father Kleinsorge comforts many of the dying and wounded, even as he falls prey to radiation sickness. He helps Miss Sasaki recover her will to live and eventually become a nun. In the years after the war, he becomes a Japanese citizen and takes the name Father Makoto Takakura.

Toshiko Sasaki A young clerk who works in a tin works factory. Miss Sasaki becomes trapped in the wreckage of a factory when a bookcase crashes onto her. For weeks she receives no real medical care for her leg, which is badly fractured and infected, and she remains crippled for the rest of her life. After the war, with the guidance of Father Kleinsorge, she becomes a nun, Sister Dominique Sasaki.

Dr. Masakazu Fujii A physician whose clinic topples into the water when the bomb strikes. He, like other doctors in Hiroshima, is too badly injured to help anybody else. Though apparently unaffected by radiation, he falls victim to a sudden, mysterious illness years later.

Reverend Mr. Kiyoshi Tanimoto A Methodist pastor living in Hiroshima. Mr. Kiyoshi helps bring many of the nameless dying and wounded to safety as fires rage around the city. In the years following the war, he becomes a staunch peace activist and tours America giving speeches and appearing on television.

Toshio Nakamura The ten-year-old son of Mrs. Nakamura. Toshio has terrible dreams following the death of his friend in the explosion. He also delivers the final words of the original edition, a school report about the day the bomb dropped.

Father Schiffer and Father LaSalle Two Jesuit priests who are badly injured in the blast and have to be evacuated, with the help of Father Kleinsorge and Mr. Tanimoto.

Father Cieslik Another Jesuit priest who helps the others get medical attention. He also locates the mother of the Kataoka children.

Mr. Yoshida The former head of the Nobori-cho Neighborhood Association. Mr. Yoshida once boasted that fire would never come to his neighborhood. He is pinned by the wreckage of his house but manages to free himself. His hair turns white two months later.

Mr. Tanaka A man who hates all Christians and who accuses Mr. Tanimoto of being an American spy. Mr. Tanimoto reads Mr. Tanaka a psalm on his deathbed.

Mrs. Kamai Mr. Tanimoto's next-door neighbor. After the explosion, she walks around for days, clutching her dead baby in her arms and desperately pleading with Mr. Tanimoto to find her husband—a missing, presumably dead, soldier.

The Kataoka children A young brother and sister who believe they have lost their family. They are comforted by Father Kleinsorge and Father Cieslik for weeks until they are finally reunited with their mother.

Mr. Fukai The secretary of the diocese at the Jesuit mission. Father Kleinsorge carries Mr. Fukai out of the mission on his back, but Mr. Fukai escapes and returns to throw himself into the flames.

Father Siemes A Jesuit priest who writes a report for the Holy See in Rome about the atomic bomb. He expresses mixed views about the morality of using such a powerful weapon.

Satsue Yoshiki A young woman who becomes Father Kleinsorge's cook, nurse, and close friend in the years leading up to his death.

Hiroshima Maidens A group of young, unmarried women in Hiroshima whose faces are so badly burned from the explosion that many people, including Mr. Tanimoto, help them receive plastic surgery.

Norman Cousins A prominent American editor. Mr. Cousins orchestrates many of Mr. Tanimoto's speeches and appearances in America in the postwar years.

Pearl Buck A prominent American author who befriends Mr. Tanimoto. She is the author of *The Good Earth*.

Koko Tanimoto The daughter of Mr. Tanimoto. Koko is exposed to radiation as a baby during the explosion and is unable to have children when she grows up.

Shigeyuki Fujii One of Dr. Fujii's sons. Shigeyuki finds Dr. Fujii poisoned by gas leaking out of his heater in 1963.

ANALYSIS OF MAJOR CHARACTERS

MRS. HATSUYO NAKAMURA

A tailor's widow raising three young children on her own, Mrs. Nakamura is caring and resourceful, as well as a dedicated citizen. As Hersey puts it, she "had long had a habit of doing as she was told." She and her children survive the explosion without any external physical harm, but she and her daughter, Myeko, later come down with radiation sickness and suffer with it for years.

Of the six people profiled in *Hiroshima,* Mrs. Nakamura is the only one in charge of a family—although some of the male characters are married, their wives and children are not present in the narrative—and the only person who struggles with poverty as a direct result of the war. Perhaps because she is busy caring for herself and her children after the bombing, as opposed to being involved with the larger community, she never emerges as a clearly defined character. We get a glimpse into her psyche when, in Chapter Four, Hersey says that after hearing that they poisoned the city, she begins to hate America even more than she did during the war. When this rumor is later dispelled, however, she returns to an attitude of general passivity, summing up her position regarding the war with the expression "*Shikata ga nai,*" or "It can't be helped."

Mrs. Nakamura's role in the narrative seems to be that of an ordinary victim of an extraordinary event. She suffers from radiation sickness and, consequently, extreme poverty, for many years—yet she does not harbor hatred or resentment about her predicament. She eventually manages to get a good job, and when we last see her she is financially well off and content. Mrs. Nakamura shows us that even after being unwilling guinea pigs in the worst act of war in history, many citizens of Hiroshima simply continued on with their lives as best as they could.

DR. TERUFUMI SASAKI

A twenty-five-year-old surgeon at the Red Cross Hospital in Hiroshima, Dr. Sasaki is hardworking, idealistic, and ambitious. We learn the extent of his selflessness early, when Hersey describes how he risks penalties by treating sick patients in the suburbs without a permit. As the only physician at the hospital who is unharmed in the explosion, he treats thousands of the dying and wounded people of Hiroshima. Dr. Sasaki contributes to important medical advances in the analysis and treatment of radiation sickness after the bombing, and for years he spends most of his time trying to remove keloids—the red, rubbery scars that grow over severe burns—only to discover that much of his work caused more damage than good. He later leaves the city to set up a private clinic, distance himself from his gruesome memories, and make a clean start.

We are kept at more of an emotional distance from Dr. Sasaki than from any other character. This distance emphasizes how Dr. Sasaki does not seek recognition or praise for his hard work. Thus, it is a bit shocking when he expresses his anger by saying that those responsible for the bomb should be hanged, but at the same time we see how he was deeply traumatized by his experiences after the bombing. While other characters attempt to simply continue on with their lives, Dr. Sasaki makes a break with the past by leaving the hospital. This drastic action suggests a deep level of suffering and a desperate need to forget what he experienced. Hersey illustrates Dr. Sasaki's emotional disengagement from the bomb victims with a memorable turn of phrase: "He lived enclosed in the present tense."

FATHER WILHELM KLEINSORGE

A German Jesuit priest living in Hiroshima, Father Kleinsorge selflessly comforts many of the dying and wounded in the immediate aftermath of the bombing, as well as in the years following. While he is not seriously injured by the bombing, he falls prey to radiation sickness and becomes weak and tired, often requiring lengthy hospital stays.

Father Kleinsorge is the only non-Japanese person profiled in the narrative. Although before the bombing he often felt that he was under suspicion as a foreigner living in Japan, his experiences afterward are not very different from those of the other victims. His experiences demonstrate how the bomb served as an equalizer: all people affected by it suffered and came together to help, regardless of their background. At the same time, Father Kleinsorge gives the readers a distinct, non-Japanese view of some significant events, such as his amazement at how the majority of Japanese victims suffer silently and with dignity.

Father Kleinsorge's life does not drastically change after the bombing—when we first meet him, he is already physically weak from the wartime diet—but he does become so enamored with the Japanese that he decides to become a citizen himself, taking the name Father Makoto Takakura. This unexpected gesture reflects positively on the Japanese people, and also symbolizes the community strength and dedication that came about in response to the bombing.

TOSHIKO SASAKI

Miss Sasaki is a twenty-year-old clerk who works hard to take care of her siblings and parents. The bomb collapses the factory where she works, and she becomes pinned underneath a bookcase that crushes her leg. For weeks she receives no real medical care for her badly fractured and infected leg, and she remains crippled for the rest of her life. After the war she suffers greatly as a bomb victim and a cripple. Her fiancé abandons her, and she is scarred emotionally as well as physically. After Father Kleinsorge encourages her to convert to Christianity and become a nun, she has a distinguished career, travels around the world, and becomes optimistic about her future.

Miss Sasaki comes closest to representing the many nameless, wounded survivors of the bomb. Several doctors treat her callously; because her injury is severe but not mortal or mysterious, she garners very little sympathy from anyone. She is completely immobilized, so she does not become involved in the communal efforts that most of the other characters take part in. As a result, she suffers mostly in isolation.

DR. MASAKAZU FUJII

A successful physician, Dr. Fujii owns a small, private medical clinic and has a wife who lives in Osaka. When the bomb strikes, his entire clinic topples into the water. Dr. Fujii rebuilds his Hiroshima clinic in 1948 and has a successful career mainly treating and socializing with members of the American occupation. He drinks, plays golf, and studies languages.

Dr. Fujii's life changes very little as a result of the bombing. His injuries heal and he is able to continue his profession comfortably and lucratively. Of all the characters, however, his life ends under the worst circumstances. He dies after being in a coma for eleven years, with his family in discord. Hersey notes that his wife and son squabble over his inheritance after his death, leading to a lawsuit.

REVEREND MR. KIYOSHI TANIMOTO

A thoughtful and kind Methodist pastor, Mr. Tanimoto works endlessly to help bring many of the nameless dying and wounded to safety. He is unhurt by the bomb and feels ashamed to be healthy while surrounded by so much human misery; so he spends more time and energy than any other character helping the wounded. He is later affected by radiation sickness and he loses much of his vitality and energy. After the war, he travels to America to give speeches and raise money for a peace center in Japan. He lavishes praise on the American people and government, calling them generous and "the greatest civilization in human history." His newfound popularity ends up backfiring, as many in both Japan and America consider him a publicity seeker. Ironically, because of all the time he spends in the U.S., he ends up missing out on the development of a grassroots Japanese peace movement in which he does not get to play any part.

Of the six people profiled in *Hiroshima,* Mr. Tanimoto comes across as the most complex and difficult to understand. With his dedicated hard work in the days after the bombing, he seems to embody the personal humility and group-consciousness characteristic of Japanese culture. Yet at the same time, his actions seem very self-conscious because he, of all the characters, feels the strongest ties to America, ties that he knows cause suspicion. The pressure he feels to prove his loyalty to Japan reveals an important cultural dynamic at the time: Japanese citizens with foreign ties were even more suspect than actual foreigners such as Father Kleinsorge. As a Japanese man with ties to America, Mr. Tanimoto feels a constant guilt and drive to prove his loyalty. Despite all his hard work, however, Mr. Tanimoto fails to achieve the respect he craves from the Japanese, and his sycophantic praise of the Americans not only seems insincere, but also causes governmental suspicion.

Of all the characters, Mr. Tanimoto undergoes the most drastic postwar lifestyle changes, constantly traveling around the U.S., appearing on television, and trying to start his peace center. Hersey spends more time writing about him than about anyone else, and he ends the narrative with a description of an aging Mr. Tanimoto in his comfortable, modern home. Mr. Tanimoto's life could serve as a twentieth-century political allegory of what happens when good intentions are coupled with miscalculated methods and an exaggerated need to please.

CHARACTER ANALYSIS

THEMES, MOTIFS & SYMBOLS

THEMES

Themes are the fundamental and often universal ideas explored in a literary work.

COMMUNITY SURVIVAL IN THE FACE OF MASS DESTRUCTION

Part of John Hersey's goal in writing *Hiroshima* was to show that there was no unified political or national response to the bombing of Hiroshima, but that there was one definite effect on the people affected by it: they came together as a community. As Hersey states in Chapter Four, "One feeling they did seem to share, however, was a curious kind of elated community spirit . . . a pride in the way they and their fellow-survivors had stood up to a dreadful ordeal." This community spirit pervades the book, most likely because Hersey chooses to emphasize it over other things. For example, very few of the situations Hersey describes revolve around families. Aside from the few mothers and children who are featured (the Nakamuras, the motherless Kataoka children, Mrs. Kamai and her dead baby), most of the people whom we encounter are on their own. The characters who have families do not live with them; Dr. Fujii's wife, for example, lives in Osaka. However, we do read about people taking care of one another on the riverbank at Asano Park and in the East Parade Ground, providing water, food, and comfort as though they were family. Since the bomb destroyed real families and homes, the citizens of Hiroshima are forced to come together and make a new kind of family. Father Kleinsorge, whose birth family is presumably back in Germany, creates a family out of his companionship with his fellow priests and later, with Miss Sasaki, the Nakamuras, the Kataoka children and many other people he encounters in the period following the bombing.

JAPANESE STOICISM AND PERSONAL SUBMISSION

Although the people of Hiroshima come together as a community in response to the bombing, as victims, they suffer alone. Many references throughout the book depict how the people have severe, hideous injuries but do not complain or cry out; they suffer silently. Hersey suggests that this is a uniquely Japanese characteristic—that Japanese individuals attach great importance to not disturbing the larger group and do not call attention to their own needs or pain. The book relates that thousands of people die all around, and yet no one expresses anger or calls for retribution. Father Kleinsorge, a foreigner, is especially amazed by this attitude in Chapter Two: ". . . the silence in the grove by the river, where hundreds of gruesomely wounded suffered together, was one of the most dreadful and awesome phenomena of his whole existence." We witness this attitude with Mr. Tanimoto, who is unharmed and runs through the city in search of his wife and child. As he passes the masses of injured people he apologizes to them for not suffering more himself. In the stories he shares later in Chapter Four, he cites a few people, including thirteen-year-old girls, who died with noble visions that they were sacrificed for their country, and were not concerned for themselves or bitter over their unlucky fate. This stoicism becomes a major source of pride for the Japanese people—they could be strong and supportive of their country and receive whatever hardship they were given with powerful silence.

THE UNNATURAL POWER OF THE BOMB

Hiroshima testifies to the unnatural, unbelievable power of the atomic bomb. The bomb turns day into night, conjures up rain and winds, and destroys beings from the inside as well as from the outside. When the Japanese learn how the bomb was created—by releasing the power inside an atom—they call it the *genshi bakudan,* or original child bomb. This name seems to recall the bomb's biological rather than man-made origin, emphasizing that when men made this bomb they were dealing with forces far beyond their own power. When Miss Sasaki notices the new, lush greenery growing up through the ruins in Chapter Four it "[gives] her the creeps" because it almost seems like nature is impatient—it cannot wait to take over once humankind has destroyed itself and its own civilization. Ironically, the most awesome achievement of man causes the land to revert back to a pre-human state. These images seem to convey that man's harnessing of the destructive power of atoms may lead to unknown and unnatural consequences. The narrative conveys the unsettling sense that the creation and use of the atom bomb crosses an important line between the natural and unnatural world. Also, the images of the greenery growing in Hiroshima show that even if the unnatural occurs, and mankind tries to control nature, nature will regain control in the end.

Motifs

Motifs are recurring structures, contrasts, or literary devices that can help to develop and inform the text's major themes.

Death

Although we never get to know any of the people who died when the bomb detonated over Hiroshima, every character we meet inevitably has had to deal with the death of close family members and friends, as well as being surrounded by death on a massive scale. Most of the deaths in the book take place out of sight. Mrs. Nakamura's noisy neighbor is there one minute, gone the next; the severely burned people that Mr. Tanimoto helps to the shore one night are drowned by the next morning. But even though Hersey does not give the reader many direct views of death, its presence pervades the narrative. There is a constant, oppressive, and almost suffocating feeling that death is all around.

Acceptance of Life's Capriciousness

The fact that the six main characters of *Hiroshima* survive the bombing by chance speaks to the power of chance in their lives. Whether they attribute their survival to fate, luck, or a higher power, the fact is that all six were just as vulnerable to the bomb as the 100,000 people who died. Mrs. Nakamura was one house away from her neighbor who was killed instantly; Dr. Sasaki could have been on a later train; Dr. Fujii could have drowned; Miss Sasaki could have been completely crushed by the bookcase that fell on her; Father Kleinsorge could have been outside the mission house if he were feeling better. Any of them could have died when the typhoon swept through the city a month later. As Hersey presents the story, none of the characters question their fates, struggle with survivor's guilt, or reinvent themselves after the bomb. Throughout the narrative there seems to be a basic acceptance of the fact that life is capricious and random. The bomb made no value judgments about whom or what it destroyed, and the people do not seem to make value judgments about who survived—the catastrophe just happened. As Mrs. Nakamura says about the bomb in Chapter Four, "*Shikata ga nai,*" or, "It can't be helped."

CONFUSION AND IGNORANCE

Starting with the "noiseless flash" and continuing through the lingering effects of radiation sickness forty years later, the people of Hiroshima are faced with many unexplained phenomena. In the days after the bomb hits, nobody knows what could have caused such tremendous destruction. Theories are developed and explored, but mostly people are left with ignorance and confusion for an entire week, until the news starts to spread that it was an atomic bomb. Yet even when the facts are out, since this was the first atomic bomb ever used as a weapon, nobody—the Americans, the Japanese, or anyone else—has any idea as to what the short- or long-term effects will be on the land and the people. Doctors are faced with baffling symptoms, such as the spot hemorrhages, and injuries that will not heal, such as Father Kleinsorge's cuts. Seemingly healthy people, such as Mr. Tanimoto, are overcome by exhaustion; Mrs. Nakamura's hair starts to fall out; and wildflowers begin to proliferate amid the ruins. Compounding the effects of the deaths and devastation is the fearful lack of knowledge about what is to come, and insecurity regarding the future health of the city.

SYMBOLS

Symbols are objects, characters, figures, or colors used to represent abstract ideas or concepts.

THE LUSH NEW GREENERY

The blanket of new greenery that Miss Sasaki finds breaking through the ruins of the city in Chapter Four is both a symbol of renewal and regeneration as it is an ironic symbol of man's simultaneous achievement and failure. While people like Miss Sasaki will take years to heal their bodies and minds, nature is not conquered or cowed by the bomb.

THE KELOIDS

Dr. Sasaki spends much of his time after the bombing trying to remove the thick, ugly scars called keloids that have grown over bad burns suffered by bomb victims. In time, he and the other doctors come to realize that much of their work has done more harm than good. In this way the keloids symbolize the continuous difficulties the people of Hiroshima have in trying to deal with the damage wrought by the bomb. They are overwhelmed and confused by the attack and its biological and social aftereffects. The keloids also play an important role in the sad story of the Hiroshima Maidens, the young, scarred women who are taken to the U.S. to get plastic surgery. When they return to Japan they find that they have become objects of "public curiosity" as well as "envy and spite." There are many social effects of keloids: employers do not want to hire people with such scars, and people do not want their children to marry people who possess these symptoms of radiation sickness. The keloids mark people as survivors of the attack, and they serve as a reminder of the destruction. These scars are a glaring physical symbol of both the damage inflicted by the bomb and the naïve ineptitude of those trying to heal Japan's wounds after the war.

WATER

Although in many works of literature water is a symbol of purity and life, the water in *Hiroshima* is a cause of death and disease. When Mrs. Nakamura and her children drink from the river, they end up vomiting the rest of the day because it has been polluted. Mr. Tanimoto expends all his energy transporting injured people across the river to Asano Park, but many of them end up drowning in the rising tide. Floods from a terrible storm wash away hospitals, houses, and bridges that had survived the bombing. Because of these disasters the water in *Hiroshima* becomes a symbol of the invisible pervasiveness of devastation. Something that is supposed to be pure and uncorrupted—something that should give life—is instead causing death and destruction. The fact that the bomb is able to spoil something as elemental and natural as water speaks to its unnatural power.

SYMBOLS

Summary & Analysis

Chapter One: A Noiseless Flash

There, in the tin factory, in the first moment of the atomic age, a human being was crushed by books.
(See QUOTATIONS, p. 39)

SUMMARY

Chapter One introduces the six main characters of the book, describing their activities in the minutes or hours before the explosion. On the morning of August 6, 1945, all of the characters are either engaged in their everyday activities or preparing for a possible B-29 raid. Unlike many other cities in Japan, Hiroshima has been spared any raids thus far in the war, and there are rumors that America has saved "something special" for the city.

The Reverend Mr. Kiyoshi Tanimoto, who was educated in America, is especially anxious. He has recently volunteered to organize air-raid defenses, in part to prove his loyalty to Japan. When the bomb strikes, Mr. Tanimoto is helping a friend move some of his daughter's belongings to a house outside of the city center. They are about two miles away from the center of the blast, but the bomb still levels the house as Mr. Tanimoto takes cover in a rock garden.

Mrs. Hatsuyo Nakamura, a tailor's widow, is tired from repeatedly taking her three young children to a safe area in response to every warning. When the air-raid siren sounds early in the morning, Mrs. Nakamura confers with a neighbor and decides to stay home and let her children sleep unless she hears a more urgent warning. When the bomb strikes about three-quarters of a mile from her house, she is watching her neighbor tear down his own home in order to help clear fire lanes. We learn in Chapter Two that this man is killed instantly.

Dr. Masakazu Fujii runs a prosperous private hospital overlooking a river. Because of the difficulty of evacuating his patients in the event of an air raid, he has turned away all but two patients. On the day of the explosion, he wakes up much earlier than usual to accompany a friend to the train station. As a result, when he returns, he has the leisure time to sit on a porch reading the paper in his underwear.

When the bomb strikes, the blast topples the whole clinic, sending it and Dr. Fujii into the water.

Father Wilhelm Kleinsorge is a German Jesuit priest stationed at a mission house in Hiroshima. Recently weakened by diarrhea from the wretched wartime rations, he is resting and reading a magazine in his room when the bomb strikes. The mission house, which has been double-braced for earthquakes, does not topple, and Kleinsorge and his fellow priests survive.

Dr. Terufumi Sasaki is an idealistic twenty-five-year-old surgeon at the Red Cross Hospital. By two strokes of luck, Dr. Sasaki manages to survive the blast unscathed. First, that morning he had taken an earlier train than usual because he could not sleep—based on the location and timing of the blast, he would have been killed on his normal train. Second, when the bomb hits, he is safe standing one step away from an open window. He is the only doctor in the hospital who is uninjured, and he immediately goes about binding the wounds of those around him.

Miss Toshiko Sasaki is a twenty-year-old clerk at the East Asia Tin Works, working to support her brother and parents. She is sitting in her office when the bomb strikes. The blast topples a bookcase on top of her, crushing her leg, and she loses consciousness.

ANALYSIS

Chapter One is an introduction to the characters described in *Hiroshima,* providing a window into the normal lives of each in the hours leading up to the explosion. There are elements of the ordinary in each description, but there is also a fair amount of wartime anxiety and disruption. Everyone's lives are touched by the war, even in the most indirect ways. Hersey shows how wartime hardship is woven into every character's daily existence: Mrs. Nakamura, for example, has been trudging up to a safe area every night with her children, and the siren warnings have lost much meaning for her. Many people, it seems, are both anxious and unconcerned at the same time.

The other common element in each character's story is the utter confusion generated by the blast. Many people expect to hear the sound of approaching planes or the warnings or the air-raid sirens, but nobody hears anything before the bomb is dropped. The first moment is, as Hersey describes it, a "noiseless flash," astoundingly bright and powerful, toppling and imploding buildings before anyone even hears a sound. Most of the people who survive are just lucky to be in a safe place at the right time. Hersey refrains from making explicit moral judgments, but it is difficult to miss the fact that the confusion and chaos that the citizens of Hiroshima undergo reflect the United States's deliberate decision not to warn the civilians in Hiroshima about the imminent bomb attack.

Hersey's narrative style in Chapter One, which he continues to use throughout the book, is to crosscut the stories of his characters at a single moment in time—in this case, at the moment the bomb strikes. It is a short chapter, scarce on details, but the technique heightens the dramatic effect. Rather than learn a lot about each character's life, we learn only those details that are most relevant to their state of mind on the morning of August 6th. We also learn important details that will come up later in the book. Such minor characters as Mr. Tanaka, for example, a man who criticizes Mr. Tanimoto for his American ties, become more important later on.

The last sentence of Chapter One gives us a sense of the literary power of Hersey's narrative: "There, in the tin factory, in the first moment of the atomic age, a human being was crushed by books." Hersey juxtaposes elements on the human scale—a falling shelf filled with books—with an invention beyond our comprehension. The author thereby suggests that technologies bring consequences beyond the scope of our imagination. However, Hersey shows that ironically, even books, the symbols of tradition, knowledge, and education, can be dangerous. He leaves the reader with a mixture of horror, disbelief, and a kind of macabre irony about the unworldly power of such a weapon.

CHAPTER TWO: THE FIRE

On some undressed bodies, the burns had made patterns—of undershirt straps and suspenders and, on the skin of some women (since white repelled the heat from the bomb and dark clothes absorbed it and conducted it to the skin), the shapes of flowers they had had on their kimonos. (See QUOTATIONS, p. 40)

SUMMARY

At first Mr. Tanimoto believes that the damage is limited to the area around him, but he climbs to get a view and realizes the extent of the destruction. A cloud of smoke, dust, and heat has arisen from the center of the city, and the wind is rapidly spreading the fire. He runs toward the center of the city in a frantic search for his wife and baby daughter, seeing hundreds of severely injured and burned people traveling in the opposite direction. As he runs, he passes ruins of buildings, where he hears people cry for help from under the rubble of wrecked houses. Mr. Tanimoto is ashamed that he is not injured as well and often asks the pardon of people whom he passes. Miraculously, he finds his wife with the baby, both unhurt, while he is running through the streets.

Mrs. Nakamura digs her three children out of the rubble of her house and discovers that they are unharmed. She gathers them up and then deposits her sewing machine—her sole means of livelihood—into a cement water tank. At a neighbor's suggestion they head for Asano Park, an estate on the outskirts of the city designated as an evacuation area, while passing many people trapped in fallen buildings.

At the mission house, Father Kleinsorge is slightly injured, but one of the other priests, Father Schiffer, is bleeding from the head and requires immediate medical attention. While some of the other priests attempt to take the man to a doctor and dig victims out from nearby houses, Father Kleinsorge collects some of his belongings. Although his quarters are in total disarray, he finds that his papier-mâché suitcase, which contains some of his important papers and money, is completely unscratched and stands upright in the doorway. Father Kleinsorge believes God saved it from the wreckage. The other priests are unable to reach a doctor because of the fire, and so the group heads for Asano Park. Mr. Fukai, the secretary of the diocese, is unwilling to leave the mission house, and Father Kleinsorge must forcefully carry him on his back along the road. Father Kleinsorge, still weakened from diarrhea, cannot carry his burden for long, and when he stumbles, Mr. Fukai runs back into the fire, never to be seen again.

Both Dr. Sasaki and Dr. Fujii survive the blast, but Dr. Fujii is hurt and his clinic has completely collapsed, killing four nurses and his only two patients. As the fire spreads, he and many others take refuge in the river. Dr. Sasaki is one of the few doctors in all of Hiroshima who have not been killed or injured. About 10,000 wounded people crowd into and outside of his hospital, which has only 600 beds. Wearing someone else's glasses and completely confused, Dr. Sasaki works frantically to help as many of the badly wounded patients as he can. Dr. Fujii later makes his way to his parents' house in the suburbs. He is puzzled about what weapon could have caused such destruction.

Miss Sasaki, at the tin works factory, has been severely injured—her leg is so badly broken below the knee that she believes it has been cut off. For a long time, she is pinned below the bookcase, barely conscious, until she is finally pulled from the wreckage and put under a makeshift shelter in the company of two severely injured people.

Asano Park survives the explosion relatively intact, and serves for a time as a safe haven for many of the citizens of Hiroshima, who lay suffering in silence. Many, including Mrs. Nakamura and her children, drink river water to quell their burning thirst, and they spend the rest of the day vomiting by the riverbanks as a result. The spreading fire soon threatens the park, and the overcrowding of the riverbanks forces a number of people into the river to drown. Mr. Tanimoto leads a group of volunteers, including Father Kleinsorge, to put out the fire using clothing and buckets of water. He also finds a boat and begins ferrying people who cannot move themselves. It starts to rain and the wind increases, turning into powerful whirlwinds that knock down trees.

Mr. Tanimoto and Father Kleinsorge head back into town to get provisions for the group. Back at the park they meet Mrs. Kamai, Mr. Tanimoto's next-door neighbor, who clutches a dead baby in her arms. She is frantically searching for her husband, a soldier; Mr. Tanimoto presumes he is dead.

SUMMARY & ANALYSIS

ANALYSIS

The death toll statistics from Hiroshima can be difficult to comprehend by themselves. By combining statistics with first-hand accounts, Hershey personalizes the tragedy, and gives us a greater sense of what the numbers of dead and wounded mean. Hersey rarely takes the focus away from his six major figures, and through their eyes we are able to get a vivid picture of the destruction. The characters see countless homes collapsed and hear cries of "Tasukete kure!" ("Help, if you please!") coming from under the rubble. Hersey explains everything from the bomb's effects upon the weather to the types of burns many people suffered. Hersey also introduces compelling statistics, citing the number of people killed or injured and the reasons why many of those who died could have been saved. Nearly half of the 150 doctors in the city died instantly, and few of those who survived had access to hospitals or equipment.

Hersey chooses his statistics carefully; he does not simply record the extent of damage the same way a report from the war department might relate information. In fact, Hersey takes great pains to show his readers how the atomic bomb was uniquely devastating. In 1946, it was common for American military leaders to depict the A-bomb to the public as just another type of firebombing. Hersey, on the other hand, wants the public to appreciate exactly how the A-bomb was a horrifically efficient weapon. It destroyed buildings and burned people miles away from the center of the blast; it decimated hospitals, killed doctors, and blocked paths to safety; its destruction continued long after the original explosion as fires spread throughout the city.

Chapter Two describes the complete confusion of the citizens of Hiroshima, and emphasizes the fact that nobody has any idea what happened. While most are prepared for some kind of attack, the power of the bomb comes as a complete surprise. Various explanations are suggested: some believe that the Americans have dropped a "Molotov flower basket," a self-scattering bomb cluster, or have sprayed gasoline across the roofs of Hiroshima's houses in order to help the fire spread. Hersey notes that "even a theory was comforting that day." Because President Truman did not warn the citizens of Hiroshima before the bomb was dropped, either through official channels or by dropping leaflets by plane through the city, the citizens had no idea of America's nuclear capabilities.

Stylistically, Chapter Two showcases Hersey's talents both as a narrative storyteller and as a journalist capable of careful observation and reportage. Even as he includes statistics about the explosion, he never takes the focus off his main characters, and as a result we are riveted by these six human stories. Because he switches the narrative from one character to the other, never lingering too long on one individual, each of the stories appears to proceed simultaneously, as if we are able to follow the progression of the events all at once.

CHAPTER THREE:
DETAILS ARE BEING INVESTIGATED

"In an emergency like this," he said, as if he were
reciting from a manual, "the first task is to help as
many as possible—to save as many lives as possible.
There is no hope for the heavily wounded. They will
die. We can't bother with them."

(See QUOTATIONS, p. 41)

SUMMARY

On the evening of August 6, a naval ship travels up and down the rivers of Hiroshima, telling people to be patient and wait for further help. It is the first official word about any aid and it brings much joy to those suffering in Asano Park.

A half-dozen priests from the Novitiate, another mission about three miles away, arrive at Asano Park with stretchers for Father LaSalle and Father Schiffer. Father Kleinsorge is almost too ill to move, but he finds a few working faucets nearby and brings water to the injured in the park. He stumbles upon a group of twenty soldiers in the woods, so terribly burned that their mouths are swollen up and their eyes melted. He promises them help that he knows will never come. Awaiting the return of the other priests, he also comforts the Kataoka children, a thirteen-year-old girl and her five-year-old brother, who believe their mother to be dead. The priests finally return at noon the next day to help Mrs. Nakamura and her children go to the Novitiate, while Kleinsorge returns to the city to file a claim with the police. The government broadcasts via the radio that they believe a new type of bomb was used in Hiroshima, but few of the survivors in Hiroshima hear the broadcast.

As Mr. Tanimoto paddles his boat along the river, he finds more and more injured people on the riverbanks and in the river itself. He helps rescue two young girls, both badly burned, who have been standing in the river shivering. One dies soon after she reaches the park. He also takes his boat to help move approximately twenty men and women who lie wounded on a sandpit, unable to move and in danger of drowning in the rising tide. Many of them are so severely burned that their skin comes off as he carries them in his hands. Unfortunately, most of his efforts are for naught. He awakens after a short rest to discover that he has not moved them high enough and that many have been carried away or drowned by the tide after all. Completely exasperated, he finally goes to a medical station on the East Parade Ground, another supposedly safe area, where he reproaches a doctor for not helping those in Asano Park. The already overburdened doctor tells him that he is helping those with less serious wounds because the heavily wounded will die anyway.

No one seems more horrified than Dr. Sasaki, who does his best to stem the rising number of corpses at the Red Cross Hospital. He works for nineteen straight hours as the number of bodies around him piles up—there is nobody to take the corpses away—then manages an hour of sleep before he is woken up again. He works straight through the next three days, and does not return home until August 8 to assure his mother that he is alive. Dr. Fujii, meanwhile, is still too hurt to help anyone but himself and lies in pain on the floor of his parents' roofless house. Eventually he makes it to a friend's house outside of the city, where he is visited by Father Cieslik.

Miss Sasaki lies abandoned and helpless for two days and two nights under her makeshift lean-to in the courtyard of the tin works factory. On August 8 some friends find her and tell her that her mother, father, and baby brother are all presumed dead. Finally she is taken to a series of hospitals, where she hears doctors discuss whether to amputate her leg or not. It turns out to be badly fractured but not gangrenous, and eventually she arrives at a military hospital on the island of Ninoshima.

A few days after the bombing, right about the time a second bomb is dropped on Nagasaki, the citizens of Hiroshima begin to comprehend the extent of the damage and learn the fates of their missing friends and relatives. The Nakamuras stay in the Novitiate, alive but still weak with illness. Toshio Nakamura, Mrs. Nakamura's ten-year-old son, begins to have nightmares about his idol Hideo Osaki, who was burned alive in the factory where he worked. Soon after, Mrs. Nakamura discovers that her mother, brother, and older sister are all dead. Mr. Tanimoto is called to the aide of Mr. Tanaka, a former enemy, who lies dying in a shelter. Once a fervent hater of Christianity, the man listens to Mr. Tanimoto read a psalm to him as he dies. Amid all of the suffering, some families are reunited, including the Kataoka children and their mother.

In the week after the blast the doctors are still completely unable to cope with the thousands who are wounded. On August 11 Miss Sasaki is evacuated from the island military hospital and put on the deck of a ship. There, in the heat of the sun, the infection in her leg grows worse. At the Red Cross Hospital, the doctors are just beginning to get control of the number of dead bodies, cremating the corpses and stuffing the ashes into X-ray envelopes. The envelopes are labeled and stacked in a makeshift shrine in a hospital room.

On the morning of August 15, Japanese citizens tune in as Emperor Tenno reads the news over the radio: Japan has surrendered unconditionally, and the war is over.

ANALYSIS

Chapter Three describes the general mood of confusion of the people of Hiroshima—they wonder what has happened and what to do next. Despite the broadcast over the radio that a new type of bomb has been used, most citizens still have no idea what has happened. The simplistic rumors of what might have caused the explosion contrast cruelly with the hard-to-imagine technological advancement of the atomic bomb. The citizens' ignorance indicates Japan's cultural isolation from the rest of the world at that time— it was decades behind the United States in industry and technology.

While Chapters One and Two deal with the immediate shock and confusion that follows the explosion, Chapter Three forces us to confront the stark reality of what has happened to thousands of people. It bears witness to some of the most gruesome effects of the bomb, with vivid accounts such as when Mr. Tanimoto tries to help a woman and gets a handful of her burnt flesh, and when Father Kleinsorge comes across the soldiers with melted eyes.

Hersey's narrative shows how the extensive damage caused by the bomb compromises the victims' sense of their own humanity. We encounter nameless, suffering victims everywhere. The hospitals are overwhelmed by corpses, and doctors can only treat the lightly wounded, choosing between displaying compassion for the worst victims and the ruthlessly economical decision to help only those who can actually be saved. Miss Sasaki does not even speak with the two severely wounded people with whom she shares the shelter; they are so badly hurt that they barely recognize one another's common humanity. When Mr. Tanimoto is carrying the horrifically wounded people he tells himself over and over, "These are human beings," reminding us as well as himself. To critics of Hersey who feel that his attitude toward his subjects was too distant and amoral, we might argue that the terrifying images in this chapter speak for themselves.

Hersey explores both the physical and psychological wounds caused by the bomb. Toshio Nakamura has nightmares about his friend's death; Mr. Fukai, the man who had to be dragged from the mission house, probably threw himself into the flames; and Mrs. Kamai still clutches her dead baby in her arms, searching in vain for her husband. Since Hersey's account is primarily concerned with those who escape the explosion relatively intact, both mentally and physically, these small sketches of minor characters are important in establishing the emotional wreckage left by the bomb.

While the vivid descriptions of human tragedy are likely to provoke sympathy and outrage among readers, some people have criticized Hersey for not appearing outraged enough at the atrocities. At the end of the chapter, Hersey quotes Mr. Tanimoto's letter to an American friend, in which Mr. Tanimoto writes about the "great sacrifice" of the Japanese on behalf of an "everlasting peace of the world." The letter makes the Japanese capitulation seem like a proud moment for both Japanese and Americans alike. Many historians have pointed to the Japanese need to save face as a major reason for the bomb's efficiency, one that was certainly not lost on President Truman: the bomb allowed the Japanese to surrender but still keep their pride. Were Hersey to end the book with this information, the implication would be that there was nothing wrong with America's decision to drop the bomb.

CHAPTER FOUR: PANIC GRASS AND FEVERFEW

The bomb had not only left the underground organs of the plants intact; it had stimulated them.

(See QUOTATIONS, p. 42)

SUMMARY

Some weeks after the explosion, three of the main characters fall victim to radiation sickness. Father Kleinsorge is walking through the city to deposit money in Hiroshima when he suddenly becomes weak and barely makes it back to the mission. Mrs. Nakamura's hair begins to fall out, and she and her daughter become ill. At the same time, Mr. Tanimoto, weak and feverish, becomes bedridden.

Miss Sasaki is transferred to the Red Cross Hospital in Hiroshima and placed under the care of Dr. Sasaki. Dr. Sasaki notices small hemorrhages all over her bare skin, a mysterious symptom many of his patients are beginning to show. He later discovers that this is the result of her low white-blood cell count, another symptom of radiation sickness. Dr. Fujii is living at a friend's house in nearby Fukawa and is beginning to treat patients again.

In early September, nature itself seems bent on destroying what remains of Hiroshima when heavy rains result in floods. Dr. Fujii must evacuate his friend's house when the river floods and washes the house away—water claims Fujii's residence just a month after his clinic fell into the river.

Radiation sickness baffles everyone well into September and afterward. In the next few months Mrs. Nakamura and Mr. Tanimoto gradually get better, but Father Kleinsorge continues to have a high fever and low blood cell count, and he is sent to a hospital in Tokyo. The doctor there predicts he will die in two weeks, but Kleinsorge lives, his blood count swinging wildly up and down and his cuts constantly reopening. He becomes a curiosity in Tokyo, and once his fever is gone and his health relatively stable, he is interviewed by curious doctors, experts, and newspaper reporters.

In Hiroshima, as Japanese physicists make observations about the blast area, Dr. Sasaki and his colleagues develop new theories about radiation sickness by observing their patients. Miss Sasaki's infection lingers on eleven weeks after the bomb, and she remains in the hospital through November. She becomes extremely depressed, especially since her fiancé will not visit her. Father Kleinsorge, who has since returned to the city, comes to visit her in the hospital. For the next several months, Miss Sasaki seems to draw strength from the priest. By the end of April her infection is gone and she is able to walk on crutches.

One by one each of the characters, like Miss Sasaki, begins to resume some sort of a normal life. Dr. Fujii opens a new clinic and capitalizes on Japan's new visitors by treating American patients. Father Kleinsorge and another priest commission a three-story mission house exactly like the one they had lost; Father Kleinsorge eventually becomes so busy that he falls ill again and must return to the Tokyo hospital to rest. Mr. Tanimoto attempts to restore his own church in the city, but he does not have as much money as the Jesuits. Mrs. Nakamura, when her hair has grown back, scrapes together her money and rents a small shack near the site of her old house, while putting her children back into school in Hiroshima. Dr. Sasaki, after almost never leaving the hospital building in the four months after the blast, begins to focus on his own life and marries in March.

ANALYSIS

> *In thinking of their experience of that time Dr.*
> *Hiraiwa repeated, 'What a fortunate that we are*
> *Japanese! It was my first time I ever tasted such a*
> *beautiful spirit when I decided to die for our*
> *Emperor.'* (See QUOTATIONS, p. 43)

Hersey's narrative is compelling because he shows the events following the bomb through the personal experiences of witnesses. Through the eyes of Miss Sasaki, for instance, we learn that the bomb has somehow greatly increased the growth of vegetation throughout Hiroshima, and that wildflowers and weeds—the panic grass and feverfew that give the chapter its title—have burst through the ruins to give the city a "vivid, lush, optimistic green." Miss Sasaki describes a powerful image—nature takes over where civilization has been destroyed—but Hersey does not delve into the image deeply in his own voice.

As Hersey's characters slowly rebuild their lives in Hiroshima, we also learn about the extent of the damage and the blast, based on reports of Japanese physicists in the weeks and months that follow. As in other chapters, Hersey mentions these facts only in passing, so he does not distract attention from his human stories, but these reports are noteworthy for the kinds of information they contain. Most of his American readers in 1946 knew little about the bomb. The accounts of the Japanese physicists, which were heavily censored at the time, suggest the bomb's absolutely awesome power—the enormous heat generated at its center, and its ability to melt the surface of granite thousands of yards away. The flash generated by the bomb was so bright, notes Hersey, that it left shadows of buildings and even human silhouettes imprinted on walls. Moreover, the Japanese scientists discover that the bomb dropped on Nagasaki, a plutonium bomb as opposed to a uranium one, was even more powerful, and that the Americans are capable of developing one that is ten or even twenty times as powerful. In short, Hersey makes it clear to his readers that this is not like any other air raid or attack; the atomic bomb should give everyone in the world something to worry about.

Hersey's own political agenda still remains unclear in Chapter Four. While Hersey includes a number of vivid details and accounts, we should also note a phenomenon that is absent from his story: any kind of serious anti-American feeling in the wake of Hiroshima's destruction. Mrs. Nakamura develops a bitter hatred of Americans when she believes that they have dropped a poison on the city; but when this rumor turns out to be unfounded, her hatred quickly fades away. Later she tells Hersey that the general attitude of the Japanese is a kind of grim acceptance: "It was war and we had to expect it." Mr. Tanimoto writes a letter to an American friend with a kind of pride in the way the Japanese reacted. He describes a father and son consecrating their lives to their Emperor, or two girls who sing the national anthem as they are crushed under a fallen fence. Hersey notes that there is a "curious kind of elated community spirit" among most of the survivors of the blast. Out of all the voices in Hersey's account, only Dr. Sasaki seems to maintain any sort of bitterness toward those who dropped the bomb.

The end of this chapter, which was the end of the original edition of Hersey's book, includes somewhat ambivalent and ambiguous accounts. Father Siemes, in his letter to Rome, offers a detached view of the tragedy, proposing that total war—a concept promoted by the Japanese in World War II—will necessarily include war against civilians. Such a view would no doubt be amenable to Americans who support the decision to drop the bomb. Toshio Nakamura's account of the day of the explosion is also short of moral judgments and instead offers an impressionistic view of the day. Just as he has done throughout the book, Hersey lets the image speak for itself: a ten-year-old boy who progresses from eating peanuts in the morning, to seeing "burned and bleeding" people walking around, to meeting a child his own age whose mother is dead.

CHAPTER FIVE: THE AFTERMATH

SUMMARY

Chapter Five is actually a postscript written forty years after the original edition. It traces the six characters' lives in the years after the bomb.

Many employers are reluctant to hire people with A-bomb sickness in the years after the war, and as a result, Nakamura-san (as Hersey now refers to Nakamura) faces tremendous poverty and difficulty for a long time. She ends up working for thirteen years at a mothball factory, and when her son Toshio begins working to support the family, she is finally able to retire. Once her children marry and move away, Nakamura-san lives off her pension. In 1975 a new law is passed, granting a monthly allowance to her and to other victims of the atomic bomb. She begins to live comfortably, taking up dancing and embroidery, and forty years after the bomb, she dances along Peace Boulevard in a flower festival in Hiroshima.

In the years after the bomb, Dr. Sasaki spends most of his time at the Red Cross Hospital dealing with keloids—red, rubbery scars that grow over the bad burns of many of the hibakusha (a Japanese word for the victims, literally "explosion-affected persons"). In 1951, haunted by his awful experiences there, he quits the hospital and eventually sets up a private clinic in Mukaihara. Tragedy strikes Dr. Sasaki's life again, however. In 1963 he nearly dies when an operation to remove one of his lungs goes awry; in 1972, his wife dies of breast cancer. These two experiences drive him to devote his life to his work. He uses the success of his clinic to build bigger and better medical facilities, and forty years after the bomb, we find him working as hard as ever to help people.

Father Kleinsorge becomes a Japanese citizen and takes the name Father Makoto Takakura. He never gets over his radiation sickness and eventually works himself to exhaustion trying to help and convert people in Hiroshima. In 1961 he moves to a tiny church in Mukaihara, where he begins a close friendship with his cook and eventual nurse, Satsue Yoshiki. His health continues to fade, and in 1976 he falls on an icy path and fractures vertebrae in his back. He is bedridden from then on and dies in 1977 with Yoshiki-san at his side. Hersey notes that there are almost always fresh flowers on his grave.

Miss Sasaki, now Sasaki-san in Hersey's narrative, works in orphanages for a time and has three operations to help repair her leg, which never fully recovers. With the urging of Father Kleinsorge, she takes her vows in 1957 and becomes a nun, Sister Dominique Sasaki. She has a distinguished career and travels around the world. In 1980 she is honored at a dinner in Tokyo; in her speech she declares that she had been given a "spare life" when she survived the atomic bomb and she vows to "keep moving forward."

Dr. Fujii rebuilds his Hiroshima clinic in 1948 and lives by the idea that pleasure—drinking, partying, and playing golf—is the best cure for pain. He travels to New York with the Hiroshima Maidens, unmarried young female burn victims who require plastic surgery. In 1963, he is found unconscious with a heater leaking gas into his bedroom. He is taken to the hospital, and after a few weeks of apparent recovery, he suddenly lapses into a coma. He remains helpless and unresponsive until he dies in 1973.

Mr. Tanimoto vows to work for peace for the rest of his life, and travels to America to give speeches and raise money for a peace center in Japan. He makes contact with the prominent author Pearl Buck and the editor Norman Cousins. Cousins includes Tanimoto's peace memorandum, under the title "Hiroshima's Idea," as an editorial in the *Saturday Review*. With Cousins' help, Tanimoto makes a name for himself in America, gives the opening prayer at the U.S. Senate, and even appears on the television show "This Is Your Life." The producers take him by surprise by having him appear with one of the pilots of the *Enola Gay*, the plane that dropped the bomb. He and Cousins also take up the cause of the Hiroshima Maidens, although this ends up backfiring on Tanimoto, and many people in Japan and America label him a publicity seeker. At the end of the chapter, his peace center is little more than an adoption agency run out of his home, and he is retired from the pulpit, living off his pension with his wife.

ANALYSIS

Each of the characters whose stories Hersey traces shows a different aspect of postwar Japanese life. With Nakamura-san's story, Hersey chronicles the plight of the *hibakusha*, who receive almost no help from the Japanese government in the postwar years. Not until 1954 is any kind of political action taken on behalf of the victims. Even then, many people, such as Nakamura-san, are reluctant to become involved in the politics of the movement. She does not even begin using the medical benefits given her until ten years after they are available. It is almost as if she, along with many others, resents her own government and wants to make it by herself.

Cold-war politics play a big role in Hersey's narrative style in Chapter Five. Mr. Tanimoto's story in particular is crosscut with important milestones in the nuclear weapons race among America, the Soviet Union, India, and others. These facts heighten the futility of what Mr. Tanimoto tries to accomplish with his peace project, especially since the Red Scare made even the best-intentioned peace efforts dangerous. In a reprinted memo from Tokyo to the American Secretary of State, Mr. Tanimoto is labeled as a possible "source of mischievous publicity" in his efforts to raise money for the peace center, and another memo from the American Consul General says that Mr. Tanimoto might "pursue a leftist line."

It is ironic that Mr. Tanimoto is now thought of as a threat in Cold War America, since his peace project could not be more pro-American. In the speeches he delivers in America, he describes America as "the greatest civilization on earth" and thanks the country for its generosity. His speeches imply that he and Japan were thankful for the bomb. Again, while Hersey does not blatantly state his own opinions, he provides us with a picture of a country that is either passive about the bomb, like Nakamura-san, or that blames its own leaders for involving the country in a "rash and doomed aggression." Moreover, a number of the characters, such as Dr. Fujii, Sasaki-san, and Mr. Tanimoto, form close ties with Americans in the postwar years.

This portrayal is not disingenuous; it is true that the general spirit in the postwar years was one of reconciliation with America, and not hostility. Nonetheless, it is interesting that he did not find or include a single person who criticized the decision to drop the bomb, or one who still harbored resentment for President Truman or the American government. In the last chapter, Dr. Sasaki expresses his desire to put the Americans on trial for war crimes. We wonder whether Hersey found such voices but decided not to include them, or whether he is intentionally trying not to rock the boat after forty years of goodwill and cooperation between the two countries.

Hersey does not erase the memory of the bomb, however, and his notes about the escalation of nuclear development among the major superpowers are important reminders that another such tragedy could happen at any time. The effects of the bomb continue to touch the lives of many Japanese in significant ways. Mr. Tanimoto's daughter Koko, as a *hibakusha,* must have a checkup every year at an American clinic, and when she is an adolescent, she is ogled by the doctors as she stands naked. Later, she is unable to marry the man she falls in love with because his father forbids his son to marry an A-bomb victim; when she does eventually marry and become pregnant, she has a miscarriage and has to adopt. By including these stories about Koko, Hersey reminds us how the bomb's effects persist for generations.

Stylistically, Chapter Five is a break from previous chapters in that it tells each story completely, with no crosscutting from character to character. Whereas each previous chapter took place in a rel-

SUMMARY & ANALYSIS

atively short period of time, the postscript covers the characters' lives in the last forty years. Thus, Hersey's project in 1985 is significantly different from that of 1946; here he attempts to give as complete a portrait as possible of each individual character. As a result, one might argue that his style is less successful because it tends to be more inclusive than selective—he includes many random details about a character's life instead of keeping only details relevant to the experience of the atomic bomb. On the other hand, one might also argue that the last chapter is a more impartial account because it involves fewer authorial decisions. When writing the first four chapters, Hersey first had to narrow his characters down to six and then decide which moments of their experiences he was going to include, and in what fashion. In the fifth chapter, however, he seems to directly report more of what these characters tell him.

Hersey's most stylistically interesting section in Chapter Five is the final one, in which he intersperses Mr. Tanimoto's story with facts about worldwide nuclear development. These facts heighten the pace of the section and remind us of the urgency of the threat of nuclear warfare. Moreover, his inclusion of other voices—the Tokyo government and the American Consul General—provides a valuable outside perspective and gives us a clue to the kind of Cold War paranoia that can silence those who, like Tanimoto and Hersey, want peace. The last paragraph of the narrative, when Hersey describes Mr. Tanimoto's cushy life, can also be read as a political jibe at the complacency of today's citizens. About Mr. Tanimoto he notes, "His memory, like the world's, was getting spotty."

SUMMARY & ANALYSIS

Important Quotations Explained

1. There, in the tin factory, in the first moment of the
    atomic age, a human being was crushed by books.

This powerful quotation, referring to Miss Sasaki's injury after the
atomic explosion, ends the first chapter of *Hiroshima*. The image is
powerful because it juxtaposes very disparate elements. Both tin
factories and books represent technologies that have become old-
fashioned in the atomic age. Books are mundane and nonthreaten-
ing, whereas the force of the blast is almost beyond human comprehension. On the other hand, both books and "the atomic age"
suggest human knowledge turning on human beings to destroy
them. Miss Sasaki is crushed because of the misuse of scientific
knowledge, and the fact that books literally fall on her and crush her
symbolically underscores this idea.

2. He was the only person making his way into the city; he met hundreds and hundreds who were fleeing, and every one of them seemed to be hurt in some way. The eyebrows of some were burned off and skin hung from their faces and hands. Others, because of pain, held their arms up as if carrying something in both hands. Some were vomiting as they walked. Many were naked or in shreds of clothing. On some undressed bodies, the burns had made patterns—of undershirt straps and suspenders and, on the skin of some women (since white repelled the heat from the bomb and dark clothes absorbed it and conducted it to the skin), the shapes of flowers they had had on their kimonos. Many, although injured themselves, supported relatives who were worse off. Almost all had their heads bowed, looked straight ahead, were silent, and showed no expression whatsoever.

Mr. Tanimoto encounters this gruesome scene as he runs into the city in search of his wife and child in Chapter Two. This is one of a few scenes where we encounter large groups of severely injured, nameless victims of the bomb. Hersey describes the scene graphically, but he does not try to sensationalize this potentially dramatic, cinematic moment; he merely describes the tragic facts and allows the horrible details to speak for themselves. This paragraph also conveys two of the narrative's themes—that following the tragedy, the victims helped one another as best as they could, whether or not they were injured, themselves; and that many victims showed a uniquely Japanese stoicism regarding their pain.

3.   "Why have you not come to Asano Park? You are badly needed there."

Without even looking up from his work, the doctor said in a tired voice, "This is my station."

"But there are many people dying on the riverbank over there."

"The first duty," the doctor said, "is to take care of the slightly wounded."

"Why—when there are many who are heavily wounded on the riverbank?"

The doctor moved to another patient. "In an emergency like this," he said, as if he were reciting from a manual, "the first task is to help as many as possible—to save as many lives as possible. There is no hope for the heavily wounded. They will die. We can't bother with them."

"That may be right from a medical standpoint—" Mr. Tanimoto began, but then he looked out across the field, where the many dead lay close and intimate with those who were still living, and he turned away without finishing his sentence, angry now with himself.

In this exchange in Chapter Three, Hersey depicts the overwhelming sense of hopelessness that many of the uninjured felt when faced with so many others' pain and death. Mr. Tanimoto tries to blame the doctors for not doing more to help. However, in this scene he realizes that there are not enough doctors to care for the thousands of injured people, and that most of the seriously injured will simply be left to die. Hersey mentions in Chapter Two the fact that out of 150 doctors in Hiroshima, sixty-five were killed and most of the rest were wounded. Out of 1,780 nurses, 1,654 were either dead or too badly hurt to help anyone. Compounding the tragedy of Hiroshima was this lack of medical care. Doctors and nurses were either killed or injured, or they had no access to hospitals, medical supplies, and resources. Many injured people could have survived the explosion with proper treatment, but there was simply no one to provide it. In this passage, Hersey forces us to face this fact, and thus, other ramifications of the atom bomb explosion.

4. Over everything—up through the wreckage of the city, in gutters, along the riverbanks, tangled among tiles and tin roofing, climbing on charred tree trunks—was a blanket of fresh, vivid, lush, optimistic green; the verdancy rose even from the foundations of ruined houses. Weeds already hid the ashes, and wild flowers were in bloom among the city's bones. The bomb had not only left the underground organs of the plants intact; it had stimulated them.

In Chapter Four, Miss Sasaki is brought into Hiroshima for the first time since the bombing. On the way to the hospital where she is being taken, she is amazed to see that amid all the destruction there is an unexpected display of life—lush greenery, weeds, and wild-flowers in the crevices of the ruins. The inclusion of this observation provides the narrative with hope as well as a touch of irony. The most destructive device ever made by man has annihilated 100,000 people, destroyed an entire city, and changed the future of modern warfare forever—yet nature still endures and flourishes in the cracks caused by the destruction. More than merely surviving, nature seems to be taking over in a way that gives Miss Sasaki "the creeps," as though humans have had their chance to contain it, and nature is returning to take over again. Hersey includes Miss Sasaki's humorous observation that "it actually seemed as if a load of sickle-senna seed had been dropped along with the bomb." In detailing one of a number of unexpected consequences of the bomb, this passage contributes to the sense that the victims are unwitting participants in a gruesome scientific experiment.

5. Dr. Y. Hiraiwa, professor of Hiroshima University of Literature and Science, and one of my church members, was buried by the bomb under the two storied house with his son, a student of Tokyo University. Both of them could not move an inch under tremendously heavy pressure. And the house already caught fire. His son said, 'Father, we can do nothing except make our mind up to consecrate our lives for the country. Let us give *Banzai* to our Emperor.' Then the father followed after his son, *'Tenno-heika, Banzai, Banzai, Banzai!'* . . . In thinking of their experience of that time Dr. Hiraiwa repeated, 'What a fortunate that we are Japanese! It was my first time I ever tasted such a beautiful spirit when I decided to die for our Emperor.'

At the end of Chapter Four, we read excerpts from letters that Mr. Tanimoto wrote to Americans, describing the attitudes of many Japanese regarding the bomb. As in this passage, he continually depicts the Japanese as people who demonstrate selfless fidelity to their country and the emperor. Stories such as these help explain that the main reaction of the Japanese, after the horrific bombing, was one of optimistic rebuilding, not anger or bitterness. The Japanese in Mr. Tanimoto's stories seemed to embrace the opportunity to work or die for their country, and Hersey does not counteract this depiction by showing the views of people who might have been openly critical of the bombing.

KEY FACTS

FULL TITLE
Hiroshima

AUTHOR
John Hersey

TYPE OF WORK
Journalistic narrative

GENRE
War account

LANGUAGE
English

TIME AND PLACE WRITTEN
United States, 1946

DATE OF FIRST PUBLICATION
August 31, 1946

PUBLISHER
The *New Yorker* magazine; Alfred A. Knopf

NARRATOR
John Hersey, a journalist

POINT OF VIEW
The narrator speaks in the third person, focusing on the actions of the six main characters. The narrator describes the characters' actions and periodically gives the reader a glimpse into what they were thinking and feeling, based on his interviews with them.

TONE
Objective and removed; unemotional

TENSE
   Past

SETTING (TIME)
   August 6, 1945 and the forty years following

SETTING (PLACE)
   Hiroshima, Japan

PROTAGONISTS
   Mrs. Hatsuyo Nakamura, Dr. Terufumi Sasaki, Father Wilhelm Kleinsorge, Toshiko Sasaki, Dr. Masakazu Fujii, Reverend Mr. Kiyoshi Tanimoto

MAJOR CONFLICT
   The detonation of the atomic bomb

RISING ACTION
   The routine wartime actions of the six main characters in the morning before the bomb drops

CLIMAX
   The detonation of the atomic bomb, as experienced by the six main characters

FALLING ACTION
   The six central figures' recovery from their injuries and reentry into daily life

THEMES
   Community survival in the face of mass destruction; Japanese stoicism and personal submission; the unnatural power of the bomb

MOTIFS
   Death; chance; acceptance of life's capriciousness; confusion and ignorance

SYMBOLS
   The lush new greenery; the keloids; water

KEY FACTS

FORESHADOWING

The opening of the first chapter tells us what each character was doing in the instant before the bomb drops; we already know about the climax—the bomb's detonation—because the book is a historical account.

Study Questions & Essay Topics

Study Questions

1. *Discuss the role of nature in Hiroshima. In what ways do naturally occurring events, such as the weather, affect the city in the wake of the atomic bomb?*

Although a technological weapon triggers the destruction of Hiroshima, nature compounds and advances the devastation of the city in the aftermath of the explosion. For example, the heavy winds carry the fire from house to house, the rains flood rivers and destroy houses, and the sun causes wounds and infections to fester. Also, artificial rain is created by the huge cloud of dust and fission fragments that rise over the city. It is as if nature has been disrupted. In essence, the function of the atomic bomb—the splitting apart of an atom—is to disturb and corrupt nature. The bomb is able to harness the power of the elements, earth, wind, fire, and water, and control nature as if it has the power of a god. Nature, however, quickly begins to reassert its own power, as the plants and flowers in Hiroshima regenerate remarkably in the weeks and months after the explosion. Nature seems to take over where human technology laid waste to civilization.

2.   *Do you think Hersey favors some of the six characters, or presents some of them in a better light than others? Why or why not?*

Hersey possesses the impartiality expected of a journalist, and while some characters might be more or less appealing to us than others, we cannot necessarily conclude that Hersey intended to present them that way. However, we can argue that Hersey presents the more selfless characters in the book in a more favorable light. Dr. Sasaki and Father Kleinsorge come across as saints, and Miss Sasaki and Mrs. Nakamura are almost Christ-like in their acceptance of suffering. Dr. Fujii and Mr. Tanimoto, on the other hand, exist in a kind of gray area. Whereas Dr. Fujii may have been a very noble doctor, most of the stories in Hersey's narrative focus on his love for pleasure or his concern for his own fate, particularly when compared to Dr. Sasaki's progress in the aftermath of the explosion. Mr. Tanimoto, on the other hand, is a very ambiguous character. He is devoted to the peace process, but he also appears self-serving and ingratiating at times. He seems to be a leader, but he is also under attack and scrutiny for being a self-promoter by Japanese and Americans.

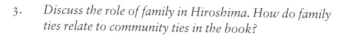

3.   *Discuss the role of family in Hiroshima. How do family ties relate to community ties in the book?*

One of the gravest consequences of the bomb is its effect on families. Throughout the book we find characters whose entire families have been killed, such as Mrs. Kamai, who clutches her dead baby in her arms, and we find those who have been separated from family members, such as the Kataoka children. At the same time, three of the main characters—Father Kleinsorge, Miss Sasaki, and Dr. Sasaki—do not have spouses or children of their own, and neither Mr. Tanimoto's nor Dr. Fujii's families are involved in the story. *Hiroshima* is much more a book about community than it is about family. Since the bomb has disrupted families and destroyed homes, the citizens of Hiroshima must come together and help one another as a community, as they do in Asano Park. If Hersey had focused his account on families fighting for their survival, his book probably would be more sentimental. Someone like Mrs. Nakamura, for instance, is the most sympathetic character because she struggles to support three children on her own, yet even her story is fairly marginal until the postscript. Hersey chooses instead to focus on those who give themselves to their community, like Father Kleinsorge and Dr. Sasaki, or those who benefit from the goodwill of others, like Miss Sasaki. A story about lost relatives finding each other or families struggling to rebuild their lives might be more emotional, but it would not have the same kind of pride and community spirit that Hersey wants to emphasize.

QUESTIONS & ESSAYS

4. *Does Hersey's* Hiroshima *focus on the physical damage done to the city and its people at the expense of examining the psychological horrors faced by the victims?*

Hersey's narrative is limited by the emotional distance of his characters; he cannot share the psychological problems that victims may face unless they describe those problems to him. At the same time, we could also argue that those characters who do face severe mental problems in the aftermath of the explosion are given fairly short shrift in the book. Mr. Fukai, the secretary who presumably threw himself into the flames, is mentioned only briefly, although such a story has potential for enormous psychological impact. The same goes for Mrs. Kamai, the woman who walks around clutching her dead baby in her arms—Mr. Tanimoto turns his back on her, and we are spared any more discussion of her fate. Other possible reasons for the lack of psychological depth are the stoicism and pride of the Japanese people and Hiroshima survivors, who remain emotionally distant from the events. Toshio Nakamura is an interesting case. Hersey allows Toshio's account to end the original book, using his school report as a kind of window into a child's mind and perspective. Toshio's account, however, is noteworthy for how undisturbed, but nonetheless disturbing, it is. Perhaps because we expect the characters to be more psychologically affected, the deadpan accounts are especially disconcerting. On the other hand, Hersey may have been unable to fully interview those people who were mentally and emotionally disturbed by the explosion, and that may account for the book's lack of psychological depth.

Suggested Essay Topics

1. John Hersey admits to having felt both "despair and relief" when he heard that the bomb had dropped on Hiroshima, but we do not know how he felt after he researched and wrote the book. Based on information in *Hiroshima,* make a case for Hersey's either being for or against the decision to drop the bomb.

2. How does Chapter Five complicate or reinforce the picture of Japanese-American relations painted in the original edition?

3. In addition to his own narration, Hersey occasionally reprints letters, essays, or memos written by or about the main characters in *Hiroshima*. In what ways do these writings contribute to our understanding of the story and our understanding of history?

REVIEW & RESOURCES

QUIZ

1. Which of the following is *not* a symptom of radiation sickness?

    A. Hair loss
    B. Low blood count
    C. Sinus infections
    D. Spot hemorrhages

2. Who or what is "Mr. B"?

    A. Head of the neighborhood association
    B. Toshio Nakamura's friend
    C. A B-29 bomber
    D. A Japanese fishing vessel

3. Which of the following does Hersey believes about his six characters?

    A. They are some of the luckiest of the survivors
    B. They are some of the unluckiest of the survivors
    C. They are a fairly representative sample of people
    D. They are fairly unified in their views about the bomb

4. Which character is completely uninjured by the bomb?

    A. Toshio Nakamura
    B. Dr. Fujii
    C. Miss Sasaki
    D. Father Kleinsorge

5. Father Siemes's report to the Holy See in Rome can be characterized as which of the following?

    A. It is in support of the use of the atomic bomb on Hiroshima
    B. It is in opposition to the use of the bomb
    C. It is unconcerned with the ethics of using the bomb
    D. It is unsure about the ethics of using the bomb

6. What did the atomic bomb dropped on Hiroshima contain?

    A. Plutonium
    B. Uranium
    C. Iridium
    D. Magnesium

7. A keloid is a type of which of the following?

    A. Scar Tissue
    B. Burn
    C. Infection
    D. Chemical used in the atomic bomb

8. Which of the following is correct about Father Makoto Takakura?

    A. He is one of the Reverend Tanimoto's colleagues
    B. He is a Jesuit who perished in the explosion
    C. He is a Jesuit who refuses to leave the mission house
    D. It is Father Kleinsorge's new Japanese name

9. What is "The Faith That Grew Out of the Ashes?"

    A. A tract written by Father Kleinsorge
    B. A speech given by Mr. Tanimoto in America
    C. Miss Sasaki's speech at her honorary ceremony
    D. A later article written by John Hersey

10. Who are the Hiroshima Maidens?

    A. The convent of nuns that Miss Sasaki joins
    B. A sewing group started by Mrs. Nakamura
    C. A group of badly burned women who require plastic surgery
    D. A group of women who work to support the war effort

11. Why does Mr. Tanimoto volunteer to become head of the Neighborhood Association?

    A. He is thought of as being sympathetic to Americans
    B. It is a good way to spread his religious message to the local populace
    C. He thinks it will help him raise money for his peace project
    D. The Japanese government provides housing subsidies to city volunteers

12. Why does Dr. Fujii benefit in the postwar years?

    A. The influx of Americans into Japan helps his clinic
    B. After his clinic is destroyed, he is able to collect a large insurance policy
    C. He starts a hospital for Japanese soldiers, which is subsidized by the government
    D. He inherits a large sum of money from his father, who died in the explosion

13. Which of the following is one of Dr. Sasaki's regrets about his time at the Red Cross hospital?

    A. A patient whom he neglected died because of superficial wounds
    B. He was unable to help cure Miss Sasaki's leg infection
    C. The hospital cremated bodies in mass graves with no labels
    D. The hospital prioritized those with light wounds over those who were seriously wounded

---

14. Which of the following is *not* a theory, advanced in the book, about the nature of the American attack?

   A. The Americans had sprayed gasoline on the roofs of houses, making the fire easier to spread
   B. The Americans had dropped bombs on combustible targets that they knew would explode
   C. The Americans had dropped a "Molotov flower basket," a self-scattering cluster of bombs
   D. American parachutists had infiltrated the city

15. Where is Father Kleinsorge at the moment the bomb is dropped?

   A. Reading a Jesuit magazine
   B. Reciting his morning prayers
   C. Sleeping
   D. Having breakfast with Father Schiffer

16. Why does the East Parade Ground doctor refuse to help the wounded at Asano Park?

   A. Because it is too far away
   B. Because he is selfish and lazy
   C. Because he is too badly wounded to help
   D. Because there is no hope for the heavily wounded in an emergency

17. Japan capitulates after which of the following happens?

   A. The Americans drop the atomic bomb on Hiroshima
   B. The Americans drop the atomic bomb on Nagasaki
   C. The Americans firebomb Tokyo
   D. The Americans conduct a hydrogen bomb test on Bikini Island

18. Which of the following countries did *not* have nuclear capabilities in 1974?

   A. India
   B. France
   C. Germany
   D. China

REVIEW & RESOURCES

19. What is *Lucky Dragon No. Five*?

   A. A Hiroshima restaurant that became a makeshift hospital
   B. The plane that dropped the atomic bomb
   C. The title of the Reverend Mr. Tanimoto's memoirs
   D. A Japanese fishing vessel irradiated by hydrogen bomb tests

20. Which of the following people was *not* in Hiroshima during the explosion?

   A. Mr. Yoshida
   B. Father Siemes
   C. Mr. Fukai
   D. Mr. Tanaka

21. What sudden change in Hiroshima gives Miss Sasaki the creeps?

   A. The destroyed houses and buildings
   B. The fallen bridges
   C. The thick, new growth of wildflowers
   D. The hundreds of scientists

22. What does Dr. Fujii do after the war?

   A. Builds a clinic for older people
   B. Spends most of his time partying
   C. Operates on Miss Sasaki's leg
   D. Operates on some of the Hiroshima Maidens

23. What does Mr. Tanimoto do in a speech given at the U.S. Senate?

   A. He thanks the Americans for their generosity
   B. He criticizes Truman for not warning the citizens of Hiroshima about the bomb
   C. He encourages the U.S. government to help reconstruct Hiroshima
   D. He pleads the case of the Hiroshima Maidens

REVIEW & RESOURCES

24. Dr. Sasaki would have most likely have been killed in the blast if he had not done which of the following?

    A. Stepped outside the hospital for a break when the bomb dropped

    B. Been working in the X-ray lab when the bomb dropped

    C. Taken an earlier train than usual

    D. Been standing next to an open window when the bomb dropped

25. What does the Japanese word *hibakusha* mean?

    A. Survivors

    B. Explosion-affected persons

    C. Burn victims

    D. Uninjured persons

ANSWER KEY:
1: C; 2: C; 3: A; 4: A; 5: D; 6: B; 7: A; 8: D; 9: B; 10: C; 11: A; 12: A; 13: C; 14: B; 15: A; 16: D; 17: B; 18: C; 19: D; 20: B; 21: C; 22: B; 23: A; 24: C; 25: B

Suggestions for Further Reading

"John Hersey." In *American National Biography, Vol. 10*, edited by John A. Carraty and Mark C. Carnes, 679–680. New York: Oxford University Press, 1999.

"Hiroshima." In *Contemporary Literary Criticism, Vol. 97*, edited by Deborah A. Stanley, 296–324. New York: Gale Research, 1997.

SANDERS, DAVID. *John Hersey Revisited*. Boston: Twayne Publishers, 1991.

YAGODA, BEN. *About Town: The New Yorker and the World It Made*. New York: Scribner, 2000.

REVIEW & RESOURCES

A Note on the Type

The typeface used in SparkNotes study guides is Sabon, created by master typographer Jan Tschichold in 1964. Tschichold revolutionized the field of graphic design twice: first with his use of asymmetrical layouts and sanserif type in the 1930s when he was affiliated with the Bauhaus, then by abandoning assymetry and calling for a return to the classic ideals of design. Sabon, his only extant typeface, is emblematic of his latter program: Tschichold's design is a recreation of the types made by Claude Garamond, the great French typographer of the Renaissance, and his contemporary Robert Granjon. Fittingly, it is named for Garamond's apprentice, Jacques Sabon.

SparkNotes
Test Preparation
Guides

The SparkNotes team figured it was time to cut standardized tests down to size. We've studied the tests for you, so that SparkNotes test prep guides are:

Smarter:
Packed with critical-thinking skills and test-
taking strategies that will improve your score.

Better:
Fully up to date, covering all new features of the tests,
with study tips on every type of question.

Faster:
Our books cover exactly what you need to
know for the test. No more, no less.

SparkNotes Guide to the SAT & PSAT
SparkNotes Guide to the SAT & PSAT — Deluxe Internet Edition
SparkNotes Guide to the ACT
SparkNotes Guide to the ACT — Deluxe Internet Edition
SparkNotes Guide to the SAT II Writing
SparkNotes Guide to the SAT II U.S. History
SparkNotes Guide to the SAT II Math Ic
SparkNotes Guide to the SAT II Math IIc
SparkNotes Guide to the SAT II Biology
SparkNotes Guide to the SAT II Physics

SparkNotes Study Guides:

1984
The Adventures of Huckleberry Finn
The Adventures of Tom Sawyer
The Aeneid
All Quiet on the Western Front
And Then There Were None
Angela's Ashes
Animal Farm
Anne of Green Gables
Antony and Cleopatra
As I Lay Dying
As You Like It
The Awakening
The Bean Trees
The Bell Jar
Beloved
Beowulf
Billy Budd
Black Boy
Bless Me, Ultima
The Bluest Eye
Brave New World
The Brothers Karamazov
The Call of the Wild
Candide
The Canterbury Tales
Catch-22
The Catcher in the Rye
The Chosen
Cold Mountain
Cold Sassy Tree
The Color Purple
The Count of Monte Cristo
Crime and Punishment
The Crucible
Cry, the Beloved Country
Cyrano de Bergerac
Death of a Salesman

The Diary of a Young Girl
Doctor Faustus
A Doll's House
Don Quixote
Dr. Jekyll and Mr. Hyde
Dracula
Dune
Emma
Ethan Frome
Fahrenheit 451
Fallen Angels
A Farewell to Arms
Flowers for Algernon
The Fountainhead
Frankenstein
The Glass Menagerie
Gone With the Wind
The Good Earth
The Grapes of Wrath
Great Expectations
The Great Gatsby
Gulliver's Travels
Hamlet
The Handmaid's Tale
Hard Times
Harry Potter and the Sorcerer's Stone
Heart of Darkness
Henry IV, Part I
Henry V
Hiroshima
The Hobbit
The House of the Seven Gables
I Know Why the Caged Bird Sings
The Iliad
Inferno
Invisible Man
Jane Eyre
Johnny Tremain
The Joy Luck Club
Julius Caesar
The Jungle

The Killer Angels
King Lear
The Last of the Mohicans
Les Misérables
A Lesson Before Dying
The Little Prince
Little Women
Lord of the Flies
Macbeth
Madame Bovary
A Man for All Seasons
The Mayor of Casterbridge
The Merchant of Venice
A Midsummer Night's Dream
Moby-Dick
Much Ado About Nothing
My Ántonia
Mythology
Native Son
The New Testament
Night
The Odyssey
The Oedipus Trilogy
Of Mice and Men
The Old Man and the Sea
The Old Testament
Oliver Twist
The Once and Future King
One Flew Over the Cuckoo's Nest
One Hundred Years of Solitude
Othello
Our Town
The Outsiders
Paradise Lost
The Pearl

The Picture of Dorian Gray
A Portrait of the Artist as a Young Man
Pride and Prejudice
The Prince
A Raisin in the Sun
The Red Badge of Courage
The Republic
Richard III
Robinson Crusoe
Romeo and Juliet
The Scarlet Letter
A Separate Peace
Silas Marner
Sir Gawain and the Green Knight
Slaughterhouse-Five
Snow Falling on Cedars
The Sound and the Fury
Steppenwolf
The Stranger
A Streetcar Named Desire
The Sun Also Rises
A Tale of Two Cities
The Taming of the Shrew
The Tempest
Tess of the d'Urbervilles
Their Eyes Were Watching God
Things Fall Apart
To Kill a Mockingbird
To the Lighthouse
Treasure Island
Twelfth Night
Ulysses
Uncle Tom's Cabin
Walden
Wuthering Heights
A Yellow Raft in Blue Water